BASIC WAX MODELING

AN ADVENTURE IN CREATIVITY

HIROSHI TSUYUKI

MATSUBARA-KASHIWA BOOKS INC.

BASIC WAX MODELING

Original Japanese version by Hiroshi Tsuyuki in 1985

English version – the first edition in 1990

the second edition in 1999

Printed and bound in Japan

ISBN4-905588-28-6

Published by Matsubara-Kashiwa Books Inc.

21 Honshiocho, Shinjuku-ku, Tokyo 160-0003 Japan

www.kashiwa-books.co.jp

Exclusively distributed in the U.S. and Canada by

JSP, Vernon, Calif., U.S.A.   www.jsp.cc

PREFACE

Many people are unaware that most jewelry items, buckles, hardware, and sculptured art are from wax models. Lost wax process casting has been around for centuries; always a proprietary process of masterful craftmenship. In 746, a large statue of Buddha was erected in Nara, Japan. This historic statue measures 15.9m and was casted by the lost wax process. Today, anyone can learn casting techniques simply by joining a jewelry club or taking a course offered by rock shops and schools.

The most challenging and perhaps the most satisfying endeavor is creating an original model, a child of one's creative mind. A model is a three-dimensional object which, when encased in investment plaster is eliminated by extreme heat to form a pattern chamber or mold for the entry of molten metal. Models are preferably wax formulated to combine plasticity with stability so that a minimum of residue is left in the pattern chamber after the wax is eliminated during the burn-out. Models of other materials, such as wood and plastic, can be used, but they are less desirable because they leave an ash residue which contaminates the casting and pits the surface.

Wax is offered commercially in varing hardness, shapes, and colors. Color is strictly the preference of the manufacturer. A blue wax of one brand may be identical in cohesive and manipulative qualities to a green or pink wax from another manufacturer. The varing hardness allow the material to be bent, twisted, sawed, drilled, filed, hammered, turned on a metal-or wood-working lathe, and sculptured by almost any tool. Yet, wax modeling is clean, requires very little space, and is performed without heavy tools. This makes wax an ideal medium with which to work.

This book makes it very easy and enjoyable for the beginner to learn wax modeling and illustrates how practical wax modeling is for jewelry design-ing.

INTRODUCTION

Mr. Hiroshi Tsuyuki has taken an innovative approach to teaching the technique of wax modeling. This book is used as a text at the Jewelry Studies Institute in Tokyo, Japan.

Too often a process is easier shown than described in so many words. This book was conceived through his teaching experience -- more photographs, sketches and less text resulting in less over-the-shoulder supervision. By introducing new techniques in each project, his students were able to progress more rapidly towards independence in design conceptions.

While preparing a model for casting and the actual casting process are adequately explained in most casting books, very little space is devoted to the design and creation of wax models.

Mr. Tsuyuki presents 11 basic projects in this book, each one designed to teach the use of certain tools and types of waxes in a progressive manner as one's skills improve. Each step of every project is accompanied by photo/ text and in some cases supplementary sketches and notes are provided to clarify those particular processes.

Paying careful attention to the photos, noting the demonstrator's hand position and the type of tool being used, eliminates any confusion which may result from the text.

After each basic model is completed Mr. Tsuyuki offers a number of sketches suggesting design possibilities using the techniques learned in the construction of the basic model.

Mr. Tsuyuki states, that by conscientiously completing each project, the student should be well on the way to becoming a designer/modeler.

Jewelry fashioned from metal

Jewelry cast from wax models

Filing hard wax

Building up hard wax

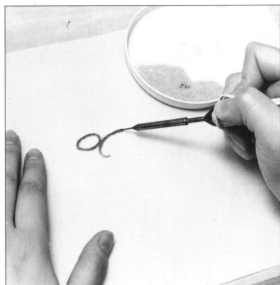

Twisting soft wax

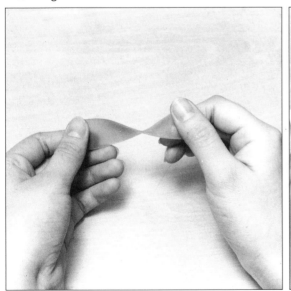

Adding texture to soft wax

CONTENTS

WAXES AND TOOLS

Start up costs for basic tools and supplies can be expensive. This statement applies to all hobbies. Here are a few suggestions.

Unless you can get a substantial discount in buying tools in a set, such as, a selection of spatulas and carvers, buy only what you need.

Dentists and dental technicians use the same waxes and tools as the wax modeler. They may have some worn out or surplus tools, such as, spatulas, dental picks, carvers, burs and odds and ends of wax sheets. It doesn't hurt to ask.

In every city there lives a "crazy what's-his-name" who claims to sell tools at give-away prices. Look for files, drills, pin vises, rulers, saws, knives and abrasive papers at such places. Don't forget to scrounge around flea markets and garage sales.

Some manufacturers package sampler kits of ring tubes, slabs and wire waxes in tubes. If waxes must be purchased by the box in quantities larger than you need, go in with others and share the cost.

To avoid contamination, use wax tools for wax only. Work on clean surfaces. Store waxes in a cool place. Soft wax sheets should be separated with sheets of lintless paper. Store wire waxes loosely in tubes or a box with dividers.

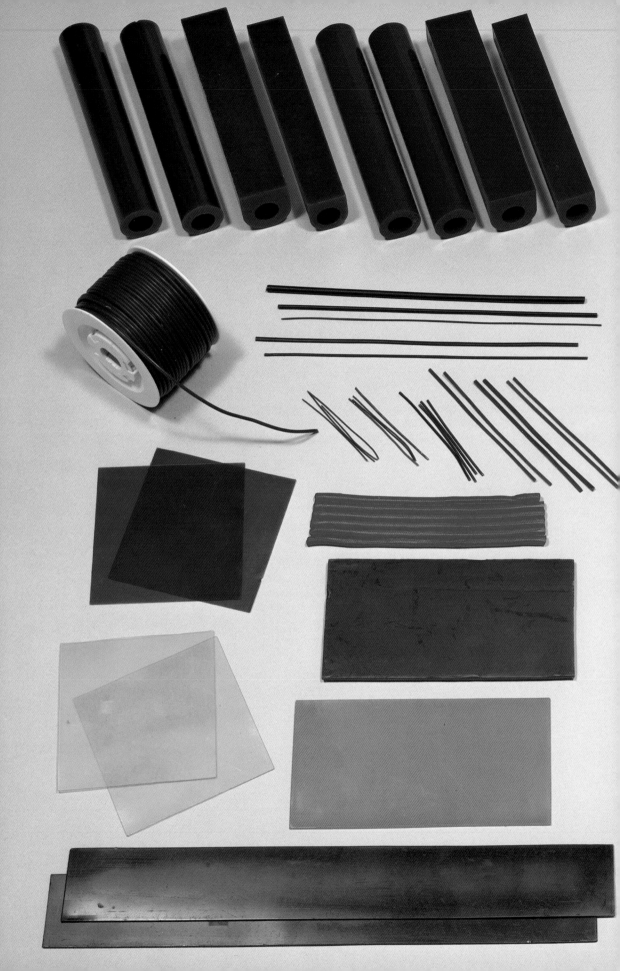

WAXES

Modeling waxes are available in a variety of shapes and sizes. The combination of waxes, oils, resins, etc. determine the characteristics of given commercially produced waxes. Color is no indicator of hardness or use since manufacturers have their own color codes.

Waxes vary in hardness from machinable to pliable. Generally, waxes are available in two or three grades of hardness designated as hard, regular, all purpose or soft. Special purpose waxes are also available.

Technical information regarding melting temperature, texture, use, etc. is usually available from the manufacturer or the retail supplier. Lapidary supply houses will carry one or more manufacturers'line; Vigor, Matt, Ferris and Kerr being the most common.

Since the manufacturers have their own formulas, it would be a good idea to try different brands until the modeler finds which brands he is comfortable working with.

Use of pure beeswax or paraffin wax is not recommended due to residue left in the burn out process or difficulties in handling in various temperature environments. Concocting "home brew" is not within the realm of this book.

TYPES

1. Ring tubes. Available in the following designations: center hole, off center hole and flat side with hole. They are made in a variety of diameters, heights and several degrees of machinable hardness. Commonly sold in 6 inch lengths, but many suppliers will have 1 inch segments sold individually or in sampler kits.

2. Rods and bars. Above comments apply.

3. Carving wax. Used for sculpturing and large projects. Available in half to one pound blocks and slices of varying thicknesses. Hard to soft toolable textures.

4. Paraffin wax.

5. Sheet wax. Available in 16 to 24 gauge thicknesses. 4 inch squares and 3 × 6 inches sheets. Hard to soft textures. Soft is ideal for tracing and cutting with scissors or cutters.

6. Boxing wax. Slightly tacky. Will adhere to itself or other waxes without the application of heat. Ideal for forming large models.

7. All purpose wax. Pliable at room temperature. Generally 16 to 18 gauge thickness.

8. Utility wax. A soft wax used to make sprues and fill sprue bases. May also be used to fill minor imperfections and marred surfaces since it will adhere to any wax surface without the use of heat.

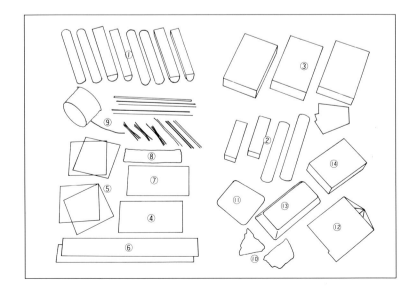

9. Wire wax. Available in a variety of gauges and shapes; round, half round, square, rectangular, triangular, etc., pliable wires, which may be bent or twisted with little or no heat.
10. Mitsuro. A special blend of impression wax, resin and paraffin wax.
11. Impression wax. A refined beeswax.
12. Pattern wax. Mesh patterned wax. Useful for open work pendants and brooches.
13. Injection wax. Used for the production of duplicate patterns.
14. Water soluble wax. Dissolves in water. Useful when worked with other insoluble waxes as a form. When immersed in water, the insoluble wax shell will remain.

Other waxes:

Sticky wax. A hard fast setting wax used for welding wax parts together and repairing. Tacky when viscous.

Inlay wax. Designed for adding onto or building up patterns.

Wax solvent:

Commercially produced solvent or turpentine. Use of acetone to stop action.

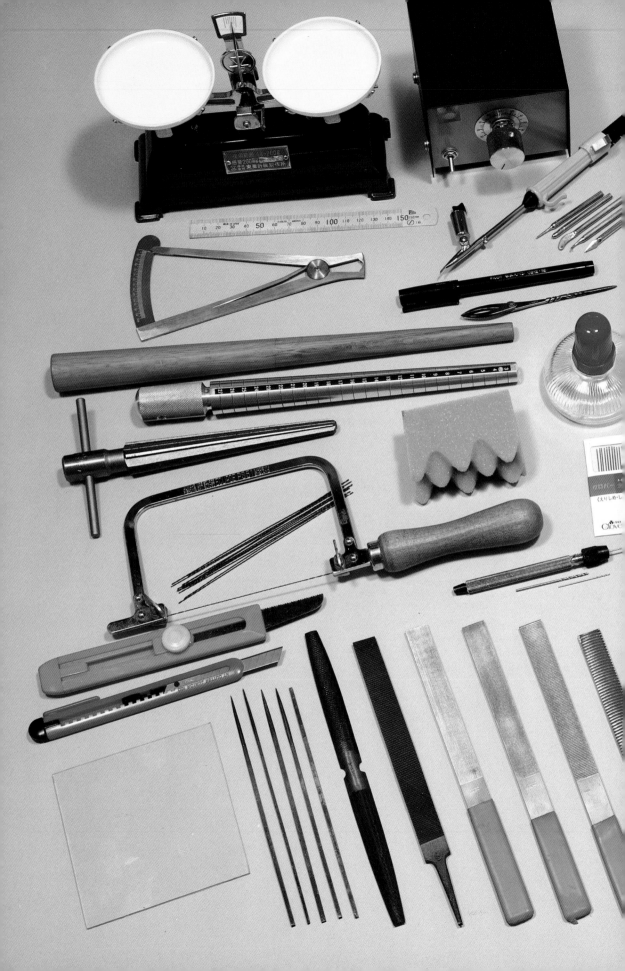

TOOLS

In addition to tools made specifically for wax modeling, metal working, woodworking and household tools may be used. Home made tools have their uses as the need arises.

FOR CUTTING AND CARVING

1. Files. Double end file. Equalizing files. Needle files.
2. Saw frame. With a spiral cutting blade (#3) and piercing blade (#4) .
3. Metal working files. Coarse to medium.
4. Handi-saw. Hacksaw type blade. Use for straight line cuts with minimum drift.
5. Cutters and chisels.
6. Wax carver.
7. Light weight knife with replaceable blades.
8. Disposable blade cutter (snap off segments) .
9. Small portable drill/grinder. Alternative: a flexible shaft machine with variable speed control.
10. Burs.
11. Drill bits. Carbon or high speed.
12. Reamer. A hardwood ring sizer with cutting edge is available. (Matt) .

FINISHING

13. Emery paper. 3 to 4/0 grits. Also useable are aluminum oxide and silicon carbide papers. Grits 220-600.
14. Emery sticks. Wrap paper around square or round sticks.
15. Scraper.
16. Ink eraser. Sharpen to a chisel edge to clean out grooves, etc. Erase light scratches.
17. Bamboo spatulas.
18. Discarded nylon stocking for polishing.
19. Cotton swab (Q-tip) . Useful for polishing in tight places.
20. Spatulas.
21. Alcohol lamp.
22. Wax pen. Electrical tool with wax reservoir for depositing melted wax.
    Waxer/carver. Electrical tool with tips for welding, carving, etc.
23. Needles. Set into a dowel or pin vise. Use for welding and texturing.

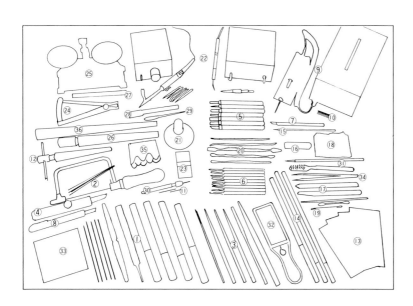

MEASURING AND WEIGHING

24. Spring gauge (degree gauge) . Used for measuring thicknesses where flat jaw calipers cannot be used.
25. Balance scale.
26. Ring mandrel. Available in steel, aluminum or plastic.
27. Ruler. With metric and English markings.

OTHERS

28. Oily marker. Fine point laundry marker.
29. Divider. School use divider/compass is fine to use.
30. Pin vise. Use to hold burs, drills and needles.
31. Toothbrush. Soft bristles for cleaning.
32. Bamboo tweezers.
33. File cleaner. Cleans wax clogged in cutting surface of files.
34. Standard window pane and 1/4 inch plate glass slab.
35. Sponge. Store soft wax pieces in the grooves. Wipe excess wax off tools.
36. Wooden mandrel.
37. Bench pin not shown. Cover with cloth padding.

ABOUT THIS BOOK

It is strongly recommended that each project be constructed in its entirety as illustrated before proceeding to one's own design.

All completed article views shown at the beginning of each project may be scaled except where noted otherwise.

Where words or photos may fail to explain a process, an additional photo or sketch is provided.

Please note that the bench pin is padded with cloth to protect the model. The cloth may be missing in some photos for clarity.

Depending upon previous experience, some short cuts may be taken.

Usage of words like "carefully" or "slowly" cannot be over emphasized.

Fragments, shavings and clean dust may be saved for future use. Do not mix wax types, however. Save shavings and dust in a double layer cheese cloth or similar bag for melting. See pg. 39.

PROJECT NO.1

A HIGH DOMED RING

Required: A flat side ring tube with hole 1 1/8 " × 1 3/8" high and 20mm. thick.

As this is the first project, the size of the ring will be exaggerated for easier layout and scribing. The ring is symmetrical, therefore, slight deviations will be noticeable. The importance in placement of guide lines and working within these lines is stressed.

Getting familiar with using dividers, sawing straight and filing flat are the goals of this exercise.

4 Views of the completed ring

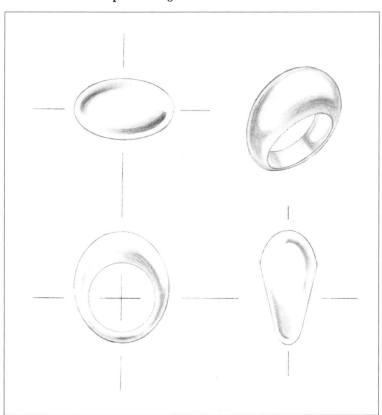

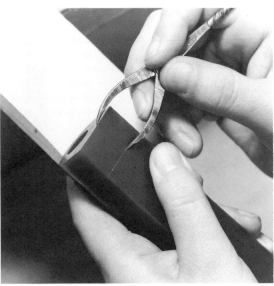

(1) Using a divider, scribe a line 20mm. wide around the ring tube.

(2) Use a saw frame fitted with a wax cutting blade-mount the blade with the sharp edges toward the handle.
With the index finger or fingernail as a guide, draw lightly on the saw to start the cut.

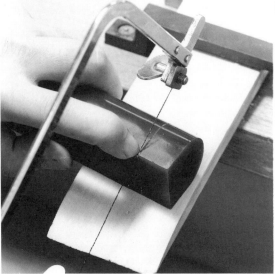

(3) Remember that the saw cuts on the pull stroke. Saw slowly rotating the tube as sawing progresses. Stay well clear of the guide lines.

Use a coarse file. Choke up grip, with forefinger ④ firmly on top of the file.
File flat and parallel to layout lines. Check frequently,

Scribe center lines. Scribe a short segment on the ⑤ flat portion from both sides of ring. If the lines do not coincide, the center line will be midway between the two lines. (See "A") .
Reset the divider and scribe a line completely around the ring. Repeat in the other direction. (See "B") .

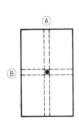

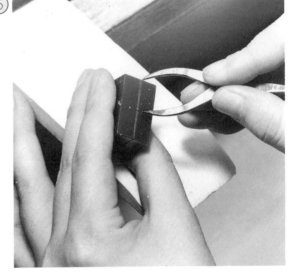

Extend the center line to the bottom of the shank. ⑥

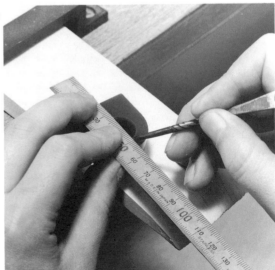

⑦ Scribe a reference line (about 1mm. wide) around the inner and outer diameter, and also up the straight side.
Do this on both sides of the piece.

⑧ Using a circle template or free hand, scribe lines as shown on both sides.
Check for symmetry.

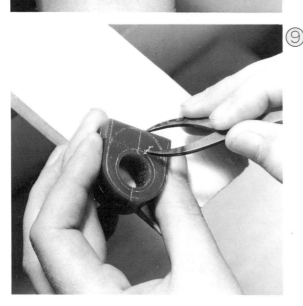

⑨ Scribe a straight line from the inner scribed circle, parallel to the top.
Do this on both sides.
See photos.

At the bottom of the ring--from a point about midway between the center line and the edge of the ring--scribe a line connecting to the line drawn in Step 9. Do this in four places. ⑩

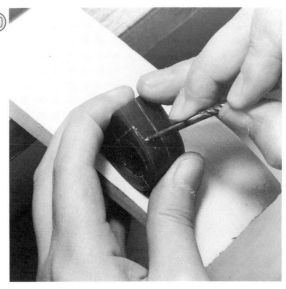

The ring should now look like this.

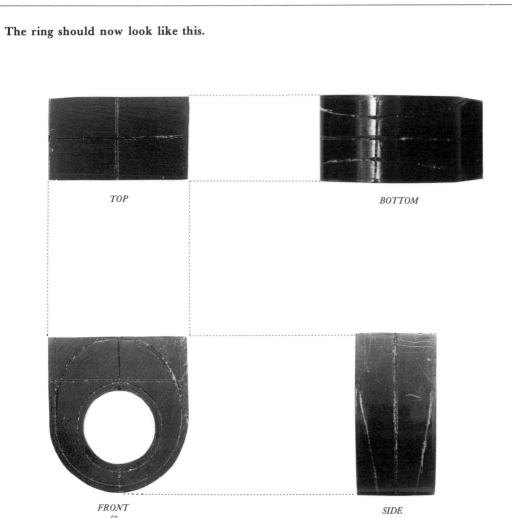

TOP

BOTTOM

*FRONT
&
BACK*

SIDE

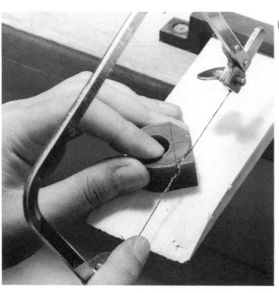

⑪ All sawing is to take place in the waste stock outside of the layout lines. Check direction of the kerf frequently. Cut off corners as shown.

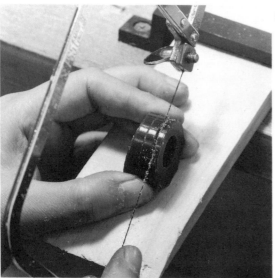

⑫ From the bottom of the shank, saw along the sloping line.
Strive to develop an eye to back of saw frame to blade relationship for straight sawing.

⑬ Coarse file to the parallel line. (Step 9) . Take care not to go beyond the line.

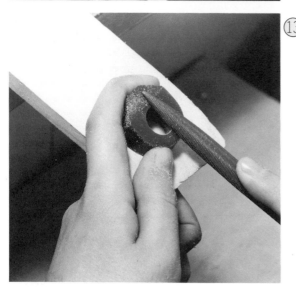

Replace all lines lost in the previous cut. ⑭

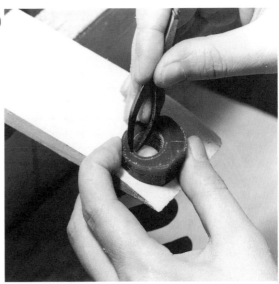

Coarse file the top portion to form the dome. File to the scribed line. The surface should be flat. ⑮

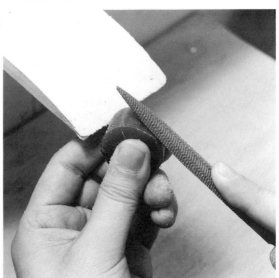

File the inside diameter with a half round tapered file. File from both sides. Stop short of the line. ⑯

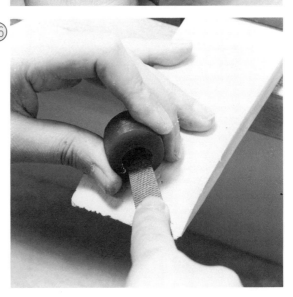

⑰ Wrap a piece of 400 grit abrasive paper around a mandrel and insert into the ring. Rotate the ring until scratches disappear.
Use successively finer paper until the surface is smooth and free of scratches.

⑱ Use a coarse file and bevel to the inside diameter. Leave a slight lip as shown.

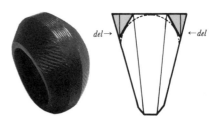

⑲ File four additional bevels.
Make a final check for symmetry. Look at the model from all sides.

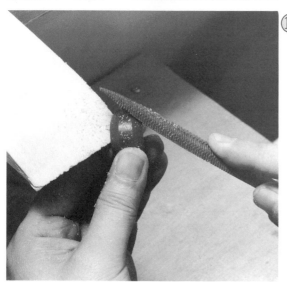

Using a medium cut metal file, gently round the sharp corners to a smooth dome.
Use a file cleaner to remove wax build-up on file as necessary.

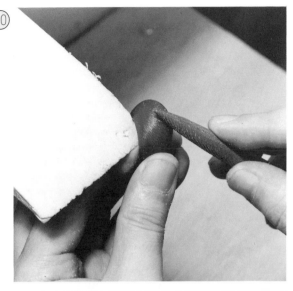

Finish the ring with abrasive papers. Break sharp  edges around the shank to a smooth curve.

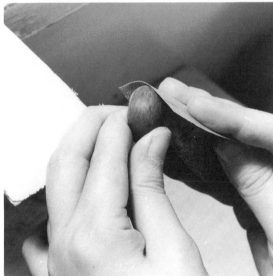

Rub entire ring to a satin finish with a discarded  nylon stocking. If scratches are observed, repeat sanding and stocking treatment.

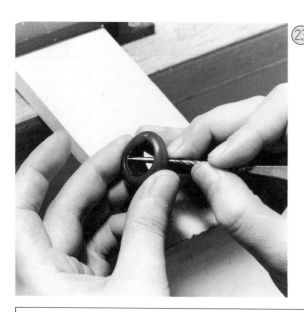

 Hollow out underside of the dome. Refer to Fig. 1 below for scribing the outline to follow.

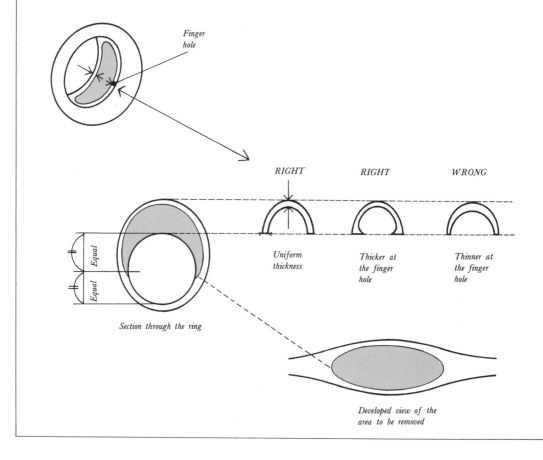

FIGURE 1

Wax removed from areas that will not affect the design of a piece will reduce the weight of a casting.

This is particularly important when precious metals are used.

Normally, the dome would be hollowed out to a thickness of .6 to 1mm. For this exercise strive for a thickness of 1 to 1.5mm. Mark the thickness dimension inside of the finger hole and scribe a long oval as shown in the developed view.

Finger hole

Equal

Equal

Section through the ring

RIGHT   RIGHT   WRONG

Uniform thickness

Thicker at the finger hole

Thinner at the finger hole

Developed view of the area to be removed

Having marked the limits for hollowing, use a small spoon shaped carver. Scrape out the wax as shown. A flexible shaft machine could be used but the purpose here is to develop manual dexterity.

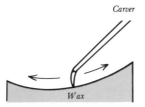

Measure the thickness with a caliper. Hold the ring up to a strong light source.
Light and dark areas will indicate relative thicknesses.

Irregular surfaces may be smoothened further by using a larger carver which more closely fits the contour of the cavity.

COMMENTS

Shrinkage in castings.

Molten metal occupies more space than solid metal. Consequently, the cast piece will be slightly smaller than the wax model. Shrinkage is more pronounced in gold castings than silver or platinum castings. The amount of shrinkage is 0.5% or less and therefore is negligible. However, in making a ring model it is advisable to size the ring 1/2 size smaller than required to allow for finishing. See appendix for ring sizes.

Weight of castings.

By and large, commercial waxes have a specific gravity of less than 1 (0.97 to 0.99) . The specific gravity of sterling silver is 10.46, 14K gold is 13.4 and 18K gold is 15.5.

Allowing a specific gravity of 1 for wax, a model weighing 0.7grams will produce a casting weighing:

$0.7 \times 15.5 = 10.85$gm. of 18K gold

$0.7 \times 13.4 = 9.38$gm. of 14K gold

$0.7 \times 10.46 = 7.32$gm. of sterling silver

To determine the cost of a casting, multiply the cost of the metal per gram to the weight of the casting. It is apparent why it is important to keep the weight of the wax model down.

Checking a model for distortion.

In the process of making a ring model, it may bend or distort. A substantial distortion will be readily noticeable. Slight distortions may be checked by mounting the ring on a calibrated ring mandrel and checking it in reference to the markings.

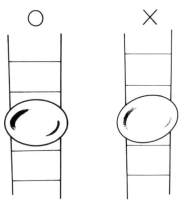

VARIATIONS OF THE DOMED RING

The basic ring

Stones and sculpture

Sculptured top

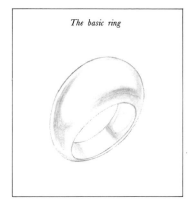

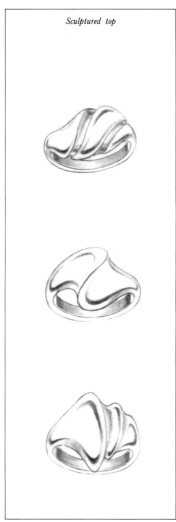

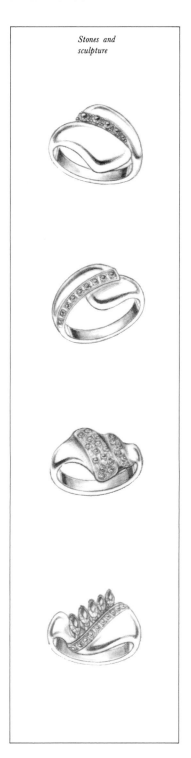

POINT OF DESIGN There are many ways to alter the basic dome construction. By removing portions in one place and adding to another; creating new designs and still preserving the basic structure.

| PROJECT NO. 2 |

A RIPPLE PATTERNED RING

Required: A flat side ring tube with hole. 1 1/8" × 1 3/8" high. 18 mm. thick.

The ripple or "S" wave configuration is commonly found in fashion jewelry.

In addition to what was learned in the previous project, more care in layout (ripples) and finishing (grooves) is involved. The complexity of hollowing out the underside is more taxing. However, it can be done. Just have the patience to follow through !

Carvers with off-set blades will be an asset for this project.

4 Views of the completed ring

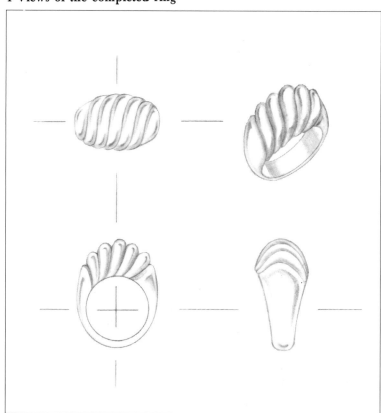

① Construct a dome ring as in the previous project. Using a fine line marker, draw the wavy "S" lines as shown on pg. 25. An ink eraser will remove errant lines.

② Check for balance. Lightly scribe over the inked lines. Repeat several times until the depth of 1 to 2 mm. is reached.

③ Using a carver or a knife, expand the scribed lines into V grooves. Check for uniformity, segment to segment, for size and depth.

Bevel the grooves with a shaver as shown. Since it appears to be a specialized tool, use a knife, file or carver instead. See modified tools on pg. 38.

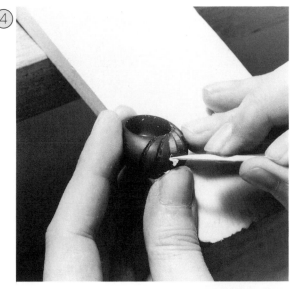

With the same tool used in Step 4, gently round the segments into smooth convex forms.

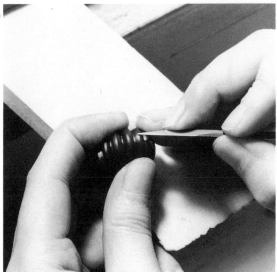

Smoothen the ripples with progressively finer abrasive paper.

400 grit paper

3/0 emery paper

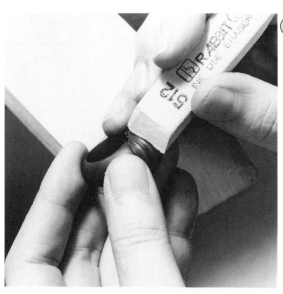

⑦ Cut an ink eraser to a chisel edge. Use it to clean the bottom of the grooves.

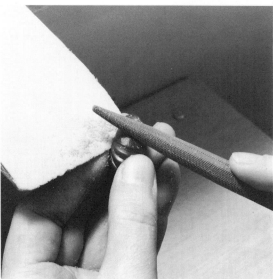

⑧ Finish the balance of the ring, fit and width for wearing comfort. Use finishing paper and polish with stocking scrap. See the side view of the ring.

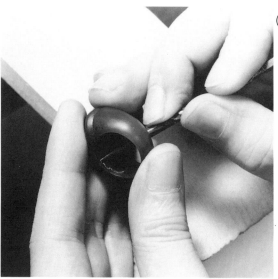

⑨ Scribe area to be hollowed out. (abt 1 mm. at the finger hole). Refer to Fig. 1 on pg. 20.

Hollow out the underside using a flexible shaft machine with a ball bur, if available. Othewise, use a carver. Caution: <u>do</u> <u>not</u> cut into the grooves on the top side. Use the gauge shown in Fig. 2 below.

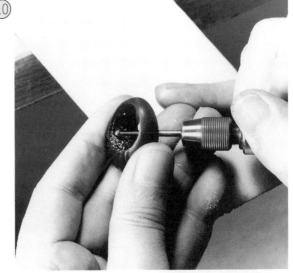

Hold the ring to a light source. Note the location of the ripples and scrape lightly until the transmitted light thru the bottom of the groove and the ripple portion are the same. Clean the cavity carefully.

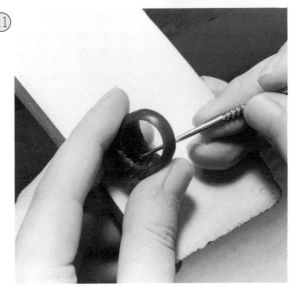

Figure 2

A wax plate gauge for estimating thickness.

Where conventional gauges for measuring thicknesses cannot be used e.g. from the bottom of a groove as experienced in the previous project, a gauge may be made for transmitted light comparison. The construction is self-explanatory. The gauge should be made from the same wax (type and color) as the article being compared.

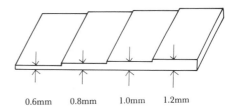

0.6mm   0.8mm   1.0mm   1.2mm

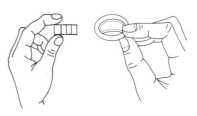

FINISHING TIPS

Scrape on the pull stroke.

Finish the grooves with a carver.

Sharpen a 1/8" dowel to a polished point to clean the bottoms of grooves.

Use small squares of abrasive paper for more rigidity.

Cut abrasive paper from the reverse side.

Use a soft toothbrush for cleaning.

Use an artists brush for cleaning tight places.

Use a cotton swab lightly soaked in wax solvent for smoothing.

RIPPLE RING ALTERNATIVES

Basic ring

Arrangement of basic design

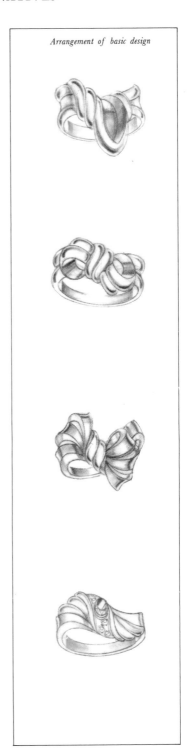

Development of basic design

POINT OF DESIGN By varying the width of the ring and the height, width and directions of the ripples, a variety of effects may be achieved.

Ripples and stones

PROJECT NO. 3

A SIGNET RING

Required: Flat side ring tube 1 1/8" × 1 1/8", 15 mm. thick.
On the previous projects, emphasis was placed in getting uniformly curved surfaces. This project, however, stresses sharp corners and flat surfaces. For practice purposes, it is recommended that the letter "K" be copied as shown.

4 Views of the completed ring

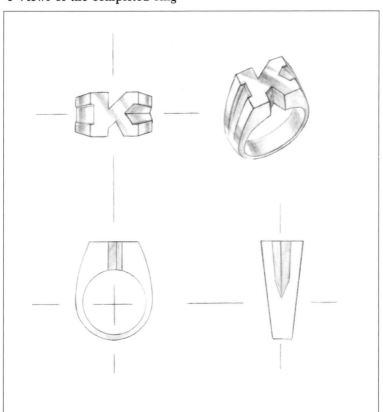

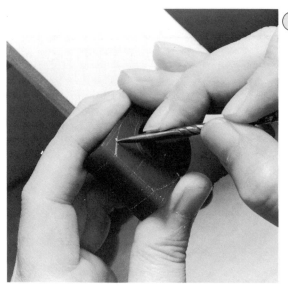

① Scribe the basic guide lines. See below. Make certain there is ample flat area for the initial, since it can be trimmed later.

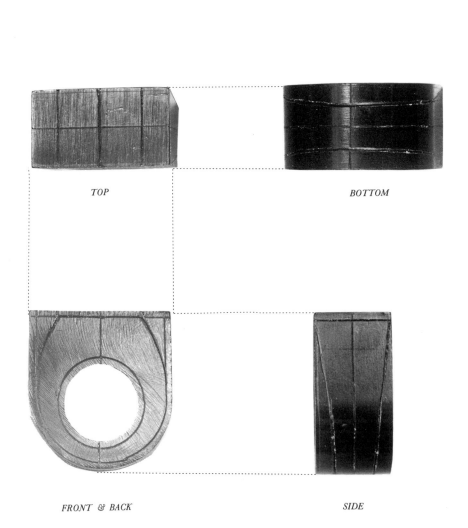

TOP

BOTTOM

FRONT & BACK

SIDE

Saw, file and sand the ring to near finish condition. ② Ream the inside diameter to proper finger size and finish to a polish state.

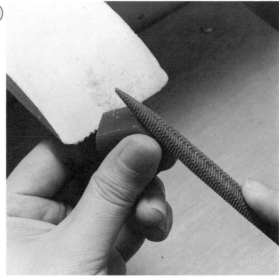

Scribe the initial on the flat via transfar or free ③ hand.

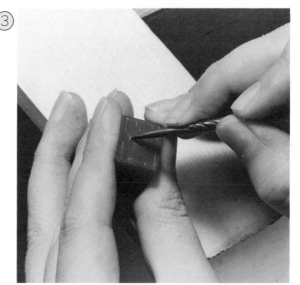

Use a file and trim to the initial outline. ④

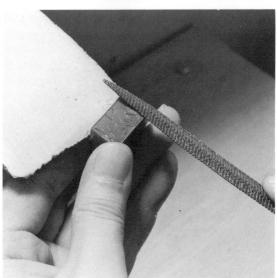

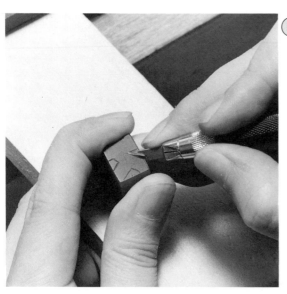

⑤ Starting from the top, cut the outline of the initial. Take shallow cuts to prevent chipping.

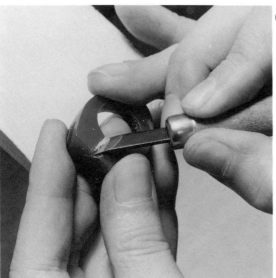

⑥ Cut down the face with a beveled edge cutter. If cutting should be difficult, warm the blade over an alcohol lamp. <u>Do</u> <u>Not</u> overheat.

⑦ A saw fitted with a metal cutting blade may be used.

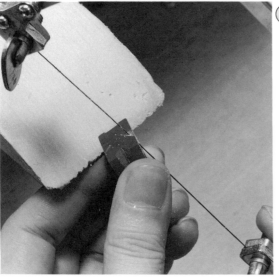

File the end-cuts with a needle file. Blend into the shank.

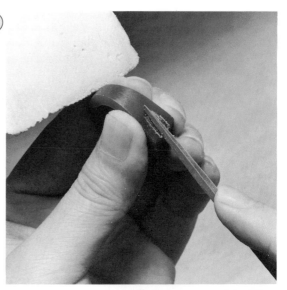

Go over all of the cuts with a scraper or needle files. 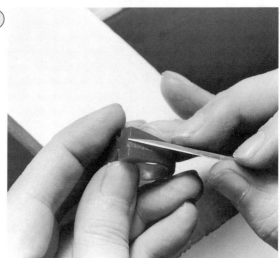 Keep the surfaces flat.

Affix abrasive papers to clean needle files using 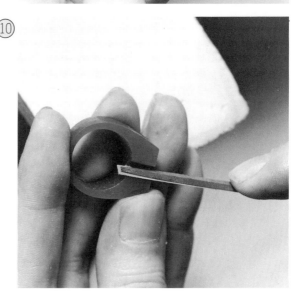 double stick tape or a rubber base cement such as weather strip cement. The paper may be removed with lighter fluid. If worn-out files are available, make the bond permanent. Fisish the nooks and crannies to a polish.

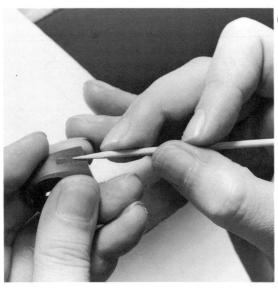

11 Use a pointed dowel stick to clean out and burnish the bottom of the grooves.

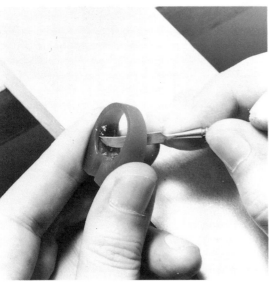

12 To hollow out the underside, scribe limit lines and use a flexible shaft or carvers.

COMMENT:

Modified carvers and spatulas and home made scrapers and shavers are handy for use in tight situation.

MORE COMMENTS:

In the event a ring is oversize, use the following method to resize the ring. Heat a spatula. Quickly slice through the shank and gently squeeze the sides of the ring. Hold until the wax hardens.

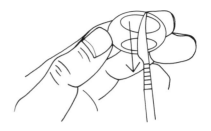

Recovering wax scraps.

Precautions to observe: Do not mix waxes (brand/color). Recover only hard wax. Soft wax reclamation in not advised.

Put shavings in a double layer of cheese cloth and tie off, leaving one string long. See the sketch. Place scraps in a straight sided container, such as beaker. Melt slowly over a flame. A tripod with wire screen and an alcohol lamp for a heat source is ideal. If bubbles appear on the surface, allow them to burst naturally. Do not stir. After the wax has completely melted, set the beaker aside and allow the wax to harden. Since the wax will shrink, removal will be easy.

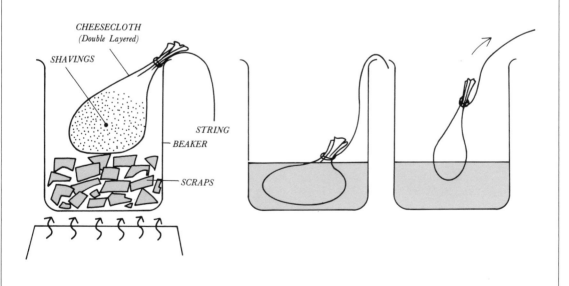

CHEESECLOTH
(Double Layered)

SHAVINGS

STRING
BEAKER

SCRAPS

VARIATIONS OF THE SIGNET RING

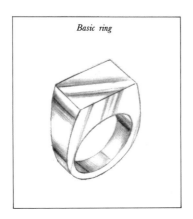

Basic ring

*Sculptured top
with stones*

Sculptured top

PROJECT NO. 4

A BOX TYPE RING

Required: Flat side ring tube 1 1/8" × 1 1/8" 10 mm. (1 cm.) thick.

In this type of construction, the superfluous material is removed first and a cap piece is welded afterward. A welding needle may be made from a regular sewing needle about 1 mm. thick. Break the eye off and set it into a pin vise or wooden dowel. Sand a flat face on the dowel to prevent rolling.

4 Views of the completed ring

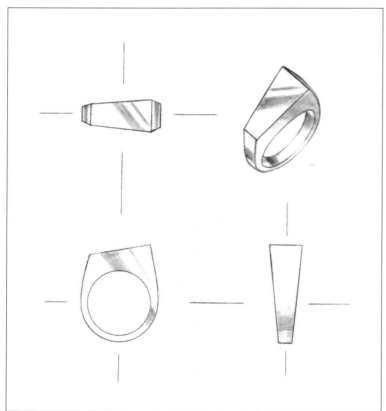

① Prepare the ring tube as described in Project 3, short of scribing the initial.

② Scribe trapezoidal lines on top: width at the narrow end to suit. Continue lines to the bottom of the shank. Scribe a line 2 mm. below the top at the narrow end. Scraibe a sloping line to the opposite end. Do this on both sides of the ring.

Ring to this point should look like views below.

FRONT   *NARROW END*   *TOP*

Coarse file surfaces to short of scribed lines. Except ③ for the top, finish surfaces to 400 grit finish.

Scribe lines on the top surface about 1 mm. or more ④ from the edges. See sketch below.

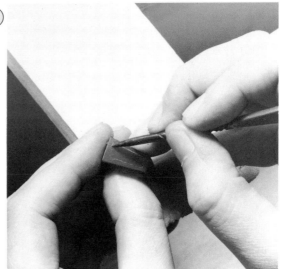

Insert a drill (3/32" - 1/8") in a pin vise. Drill a ⑤ series or through-holes, straight as possible, within the scribed lines. A flexible shaft may be used instead.

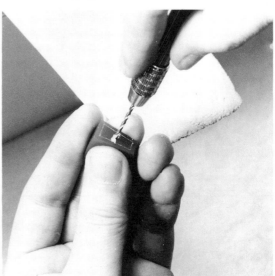

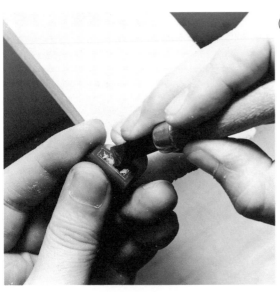

6 Use a knife with a bevel edge blade to remove excess material, working towards the corners. Shave off only small amounts at a time. Excessive pressure on the ring will cause it to collapse.

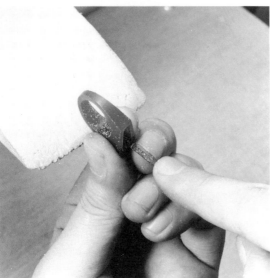

7 Establish uniform thickness to the outer surface.

8 Square off the corners with a file.

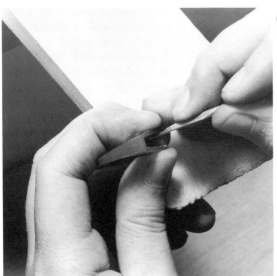

Finish surfaces with the file emery paper combination previously described. ⑨

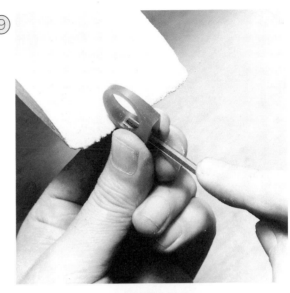

Using the ring as a template, scribe trapezoid ⑩ outline of the top onto an 18 ga. hard wax sheet. Saw oversize.

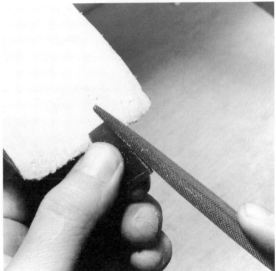

Place this piece on top of the ring. Hold and tack ⑪ weld the seam with a heated needle welder. Do not overheat the needle. Touch the seam lightly with the tip of the needle in several places.

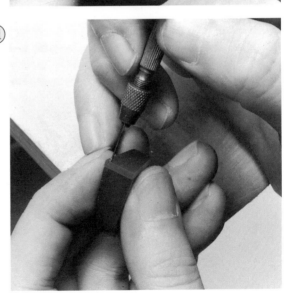

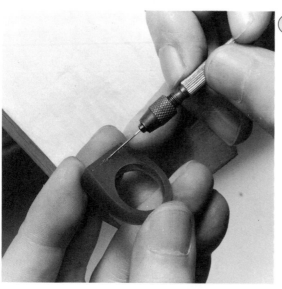

(12) The heated tip of the welder is lightly drawn along the seam. Done properly, the wax on both parts will melt simultaneously and fuse.

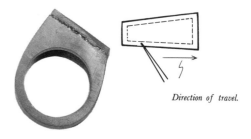

Direction of travel.

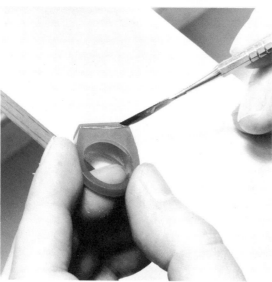

(13) Fill indentations by picking up small quantities of wax shavings on the tip of a heated spatula and deposit where required.

Wax especially formulated for joining and repairing may be used as well. See photos "A", "B" and "C" on pg. 68.

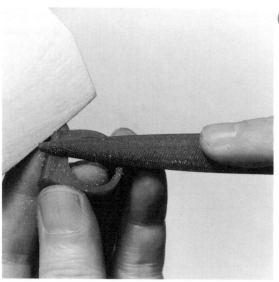

(14) File off the excess overlap material. Keep corners square.

Finish using abrasive papers and burnish with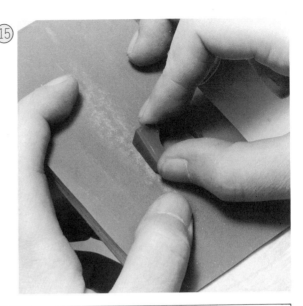
stocking scrap.

COMMENTS

Optional cutting with a saw equipped with a piercing
blade: Drill through holes in each corner. Disconnect
one end of the saw blade. Pass it through one of the
holes and reconnect to proper tension. Proceed,
cutting slowly. Let the blade do the cutting. Excessive speed and pressure can cause the wax to soften
sufficiently to clog the teeth and entrap the blade
completely.

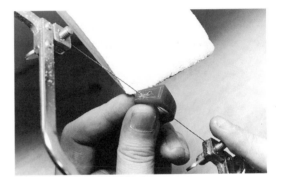

The single most difficult aspect of wax welding is
getting and maintaining the proper temperature of the
welding tool. Electric carver/waxers are available
with temperature controls and a variety of tips. For
the sometime hobbyist the cost/use factor must be
considered. A home made unit, consisting of a
replaceable tip mini soldering iron of the type used in
electronics and a power rheostat or even a light
dimmer switch for temperature control may be used.
However, one shold be familiar with electricity.

When welding a seam, the welding needle should be
tipped 45 degrees in the direction of travel. Addition-
ally, when welding a tee joint or an inside corner the
needle should be tipped at an angle midway between
the pieces being joined.

A home made alternative to the needle is offered.
Heat a large needle about 1/3 of the way from the tip
to a cherry red color and allow to air cool.

Hammer that portion flat and file to a sword shape
point (⊢━━➤). Hone to a knife edge; reheat to a light
straw color. Quench in oil or water. Finish the
surfaces to a polish with 4/0 emery paper.

VARIATION OF THE BOX TYPE RING

Basic ring

Two or more planes

Stone and texture

POINT OF DESIGN   The cap plate need not be plain. Consider texture and designs in shallow relief. Add prongs for cabochons. These operations may take place before assembly.

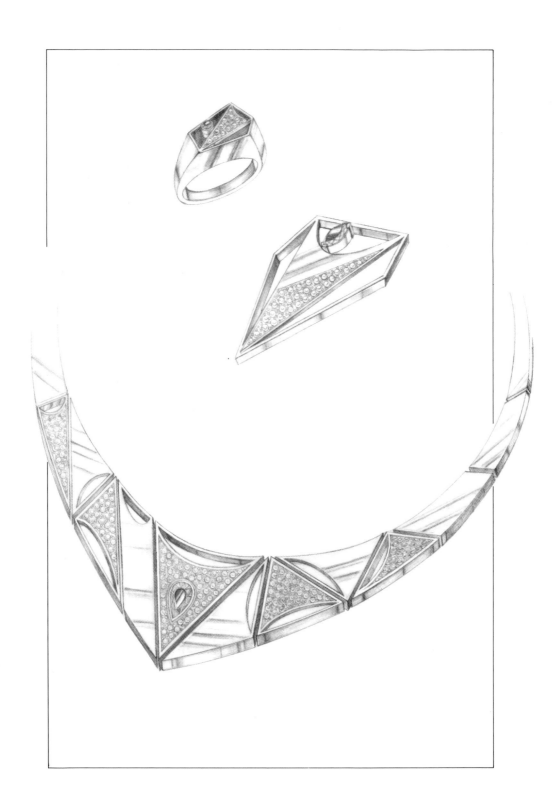

PROJECT NO. 5

A CARVED FLAT BAND RING

Required: A centered hole ring tube 15 mm. thick.
This type of basic ring is suitable for creating bold grooves and sharp
outlines in shallow relief for interesting designs.
Refererence to the ''4 views'' drawings for each step is advised.

4 views of the completed ring

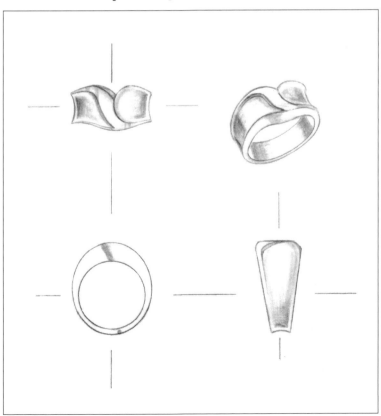

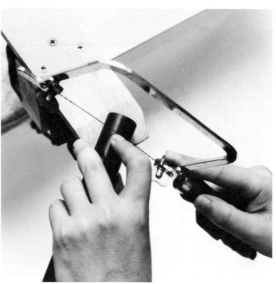

① Ream the finger hole to fit. File the ring flat to the shape shown on the front view. Taper the ring as shown on the side view. Semi-finish the surfaces.

② With a fine line marker draw the outline of the design as shown on the top view. Trace over the lines with a scriber.

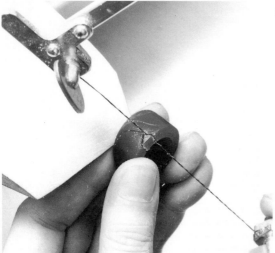

③ Cut the V groove with a saw. File the ring to the configuration as shown on the top view.

Using half round file, cut a shallow groove down each side of the ring. Stay clear of the top scribe marks. ④

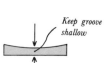

Keep groove
shallow

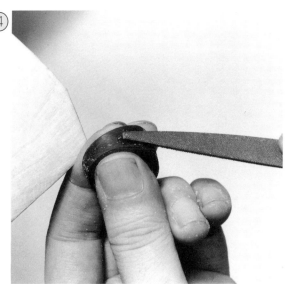

Carefully scrape away material around the "wave" portion deep enough for the design to stand out. Blend into the groove down the sides. ⑤

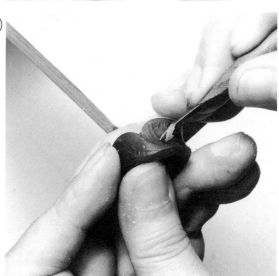

Cut deep enough vertically to define the "wave" portion. Make sure not to scratch the top of the "wave". ⑥

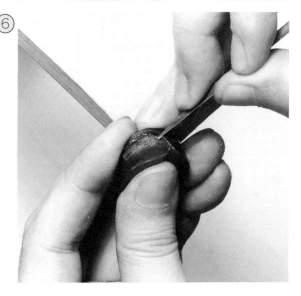

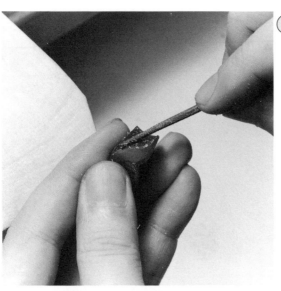

⑦ Clean the area around the "wave" using files and carvers.

⑧ Use the curved portion of a spatula to blend the groove and vertical sides.

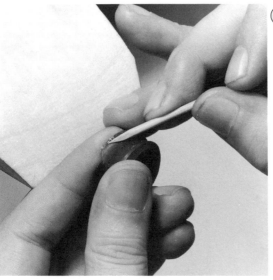

⑨ Soften sharp edges with a spatula or pointed dowel.

Wrap abrasive papers around a dowel to finish the ⑩ grooves.

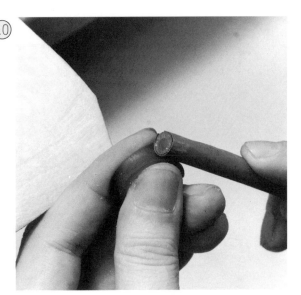

Follow previous instructions for removing material ⑪ from the underside of the ring. Hold it to the light and check frequently with the comparison gauge.

Add final touches with carvers. Clean up with ⑫ brushes and cotton swab.

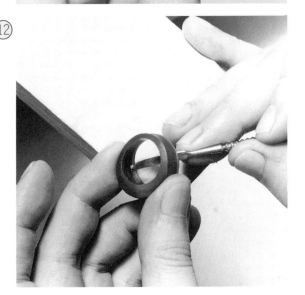

VARIATIONS OF CARVED RING

Basic ring

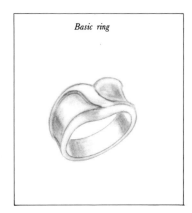

Complex designs with stones

Simple designs

PROJECT NO.6

A TEXTURED PENDANT
WITH OPEN WORK

Required: A slice of carving wax, medium to hard texture. 5/16 "to 3/8" thick.

Flat work, sculpturing and texturing are the features of this project. Open work can be very fragile particularly when thin, with many pierced areas. Develop the habit of handling such work carefully.

2 views of the finished pendant.

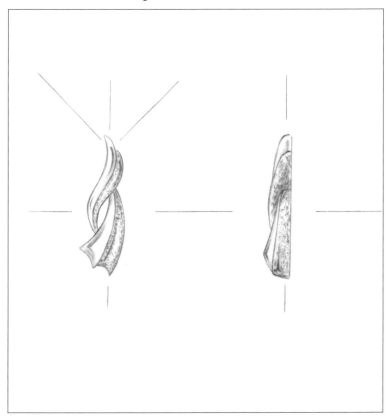

① Sand the surface flat if necessary. Trace the design on paper (tracing paper) .
Tape it to the wax surface and transfer the outline onto the wax with 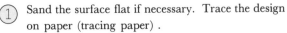 a scriber

② Use a saw equipped with a spiral saw blade. Saw outside of the scribed lines.

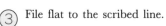

③ File flat to the scribed line.

Drill a hole in the center of the cutout portion. ④

Disconnect one end of the blade. Insert the blade ⑤ through the hole and reconnect the blade to the proper tension. Saw to the guide lines.

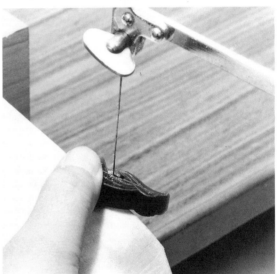

If a thicker blank was used, sand or saw to proper ⑥ thinkness.

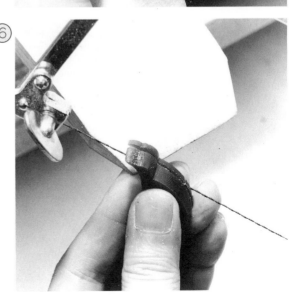

⑦ Incise the transfered lines with a cutter, lightly to start. Retrace the cuts making them deeper.

⑧ At this point study the drawing carefully. Note that the end of each segment appears to pass under the other. Cut each surface on a slope to the other. Reincise guide lines as the slopes become steeper.

⑨ Handle the pendant with care as the narrowed portions may break off. Gently round the segments with a file.

Bevel the edges around the open portion with a needle file. Choke up on the file using light pressure.

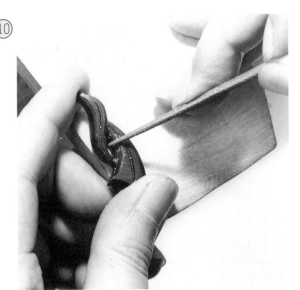

Round the segments into convex configurations similar to the Ripple ring exercise.

Clean the surfaces with successively finer grits of abrasive paper until a fine finish is obtained.

62

⑬ Uniformly mottle the surface of the segments as shown on the design with the tip of a heated needle. Practice on scrap material first.

⑭ Use a toothbrush to remove debris.

⑮ Hollow out the back with a carver or flexible shaft. Leave a 1 mm. border on all edges.

Scrape where the edge and bottom meet to sharpen-corners, Check thickness at all times with a gauge or ⑯ comparison plate.

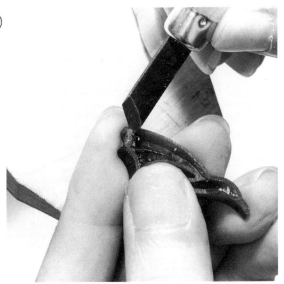

Use a carver to scoope and scrape until a uniform ⑰ thickness of about 1 mm is obtained.

Put finishing touches on the pendant, front and ⑱ back. Add the bail at this time or one may be soldered after casting.

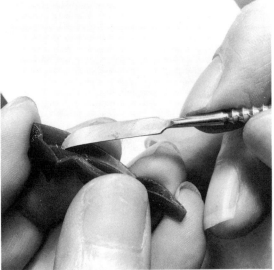

COMMENTS:

To cut through blocks of thick slices, a saw with a rigid blade is preferable.

A mini hack saw with a coarse blade will cut faster with less drift than a jewelers saw.

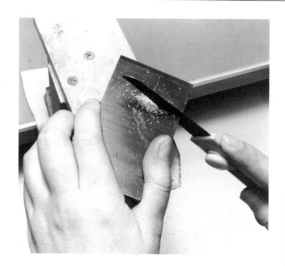

A variety of textured surfaces may be created by using simple tools. A few are presented below. Experiment with other tools and save samples for future reference.

A small bur mounted in a flexible. shaft.
Touch lightly to surface in a random pattern.

Alternate direction with edge of a wax carver.

Lightly heated brass wire wheel mounted in a flexible shaft.

A V shaped chisel touched on the surface in a random pattern.

PENDANT VARIATIONS

Basic pendant

Other designs

Symmetrical and asymmetrical designs

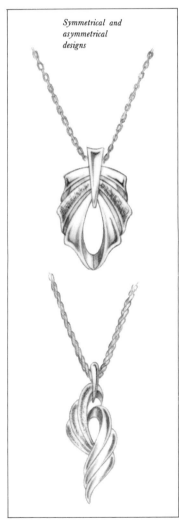

POINT OF DESIGN Forms are not restricted. Apply techniques learned from previous projects. Create a combination of convex and concave surfaces. Add texturing for contrast. Sea shells for design inspirations.

PROJECT NO.7

A BUILD-UP WAX PENDANT

In the previous project, textures were created by impressing tools on wax surfaces. Build-up wax techniques offers another method of creating form and texture at the same time. This type of texturing may have a more natural appearance.

Proper wax flow is paramount. Practice before work on the model is suggested.

Hard wax fragments and dust from past projects may be used. Also inlay or build-up wax may be purchased.

Electric wax pens are available. But, again, cost/use factor may negate purchase, although the next project will consider the use of a wax pen.

2 views of the completed pendant.

① Trace the tree design onto a sheet of tracing paper or draw free hand. Tape to a 1/4" thick plate glass sheet.

② The wax will be deposited directly onto the drawing with a heated spatula. Heat a knife point spatula over an alcohol lamp. Pick up a small smount of wax with the tip. Reheat until the wax is melted. (Photos A, B and C)

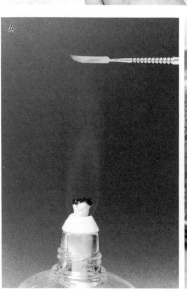

Begin build-up on the trunk, moving the spatula ③ upward. Deposit thin layers one at a time.

It is important to keep the spatula moving as the wax begins to flow off.

Wax in the main limbs and finally the smaller ④ branches.
Build up wax so that the base of the tree is thicker than the balance of the trunk.
Put additional wax on the limbs and branches to a minimum thickness of about 1.5 mm. See profile drawing.

The trunk may be textured by using a warm spatula. ⑤
Texture may be varied by heating the spatula to different temperatures.

⑥ Separate the paper and pendant as shown. Gently roll the paper in a rocking motion. If the paper should stick, ease a knife between the paper and pendant

⑦ Remove excess wax and fins with a knife. Smooth rough edges with a warm spatula.

⑧ Put a small bur in a pin vise or flexible shaft to clean areas inaccessible for the knife. Provisions for a bail may be added on at this time or soldered on after casting.

COMMENTS:

A wax pen with its temperature control and wax reservoir is the ultimate tool for build-up wax construction. Purchase of one is recommended if build-up construction is appealing.

When wax is melted with a tool, a thin film of wax or scorch will remain.
Make a habit of reheating the tool and wiping it clean after each use.

Build-up flat work will often warp. To correct this, warm the model with a hair drier or immerse in warm water. Press lightly on a flat surface.

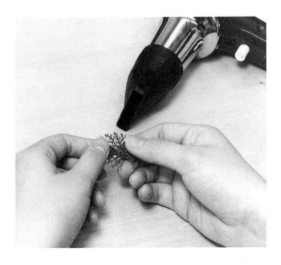

VARIATIONS OF THE BUILD-UP WAX TECHNIQUE

Basic model

POINT OF DESIGN

Abstract and spontaneous plant and animal designs may be created by the build-up technique.

PROJECT NO.8

A WAX BUILD-UP RING

This project uses the same process as the previous project. While the wax technique is simpler than cutting and shaping hard wax, it is not suitable for all designs. The wax pen technique is illustrated in this project.

Pattern and completed view of the ring

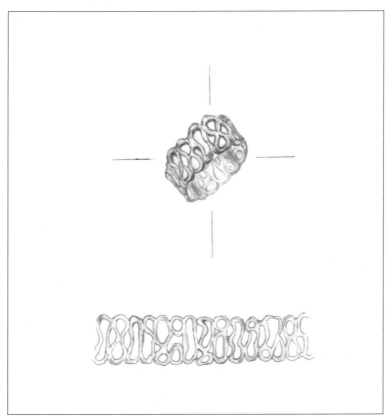

① Cut a strip of heavy paper wider and longer (finger size plus 10 mm) than the design.

10 mm (1cm)
overage

② Affix double stick tape to the 10mm overage.

③ Wrap the paper around the mandrel centered at the proper ring size. Do not taper the paper. Stick the ends of paper together.
A stepped mandrel would be ideal.

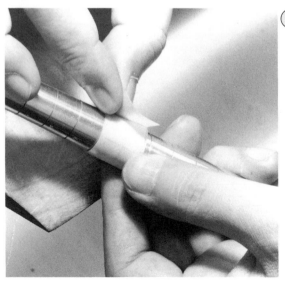

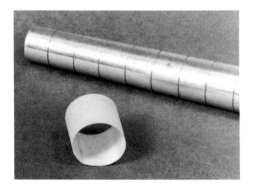

Copy the design with a sharp pencil. ④

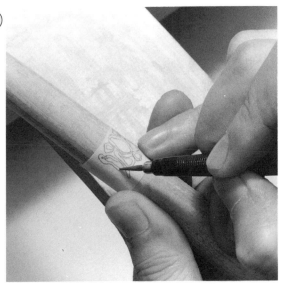

Select the proper temperature for melting the wax. ⑤
Follow the layout, proceeding as the flow allows.

Build up the wax, small amounts at a time, until ⑥
sufficiently thick. (Suggested thickness 1mm to 1.
5mm).

(7) Remove the ring together with the paper. Separate the paper as shown.

(8) Remove excess wax with a knife or flexible shaft.

(9) Pass quickly over a flame to produce a smooth surface.
A heated needle or spatula may be used to produce a textured surface.

VARIATIONS OF THE BUILD-UP RING

Basic ring

POINT OF DESIGN A variety of designs may be easily produced in build-up wax technique.

Overlays on plain bands should not be overlooked.

These are wax patterns of rings on the market. There are numerous kinds of designs patterned by various injection waxes such as red, yellow, blue, green waxes.

PROJECT NO.9

A RING WITH FLOWER
AND LEAF MOTIF

Required: A sheet of soft wax 20 or 22 gauge.

Soft wax is pliable at room temperature and may be bent or twisted easily. Steps 1 and 2 are devoted to reducing the thickness of paraffin wax. Since sheet wax of various thickness and flexibilities are available, begin with Step 3.

Note the ring is made in one piece. The leaf and flower are connected by the ring shank (finger fit plus a tad extra for the twist). Since the views show the ring in its constructed form the flower and leaf are not shown in their true sizes. Sketch them larger than they appear on the views. After bending, trim if necessary with a pair of scissors.

4 views of the completed ring

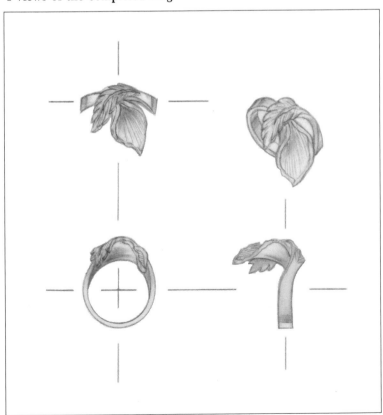

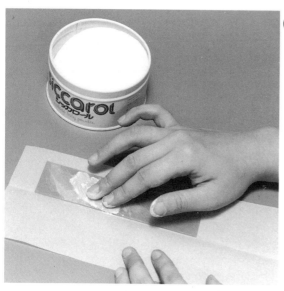

① Soft wax may be rolled to a thinner gauge if a rolling mill is available. Coat both sides with talcum powder and sandwich between thin sheets of paper.

② Feed the sheets into the rolling mill slowly. Take several passes and thin the sheet gradually.

③ Sketch the ring on a sheet of paper. Place a sheet of glass over the sketch. Lay the sheet of wax over the glass.

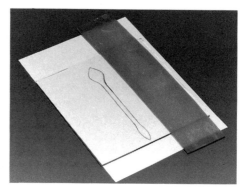

Trace the outline with a fine line marker or a ④ scriber. Cut the wax with a pair of scissors.

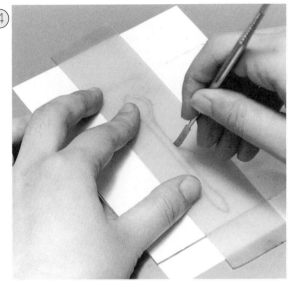

Pass the model over a flame quickly (edges only). ⑤ Too much heat will collapse the model.

Finger burnish edges carefully. ⑥

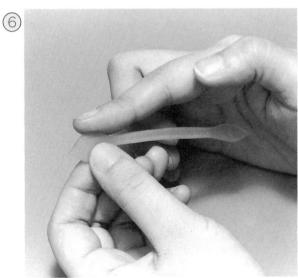

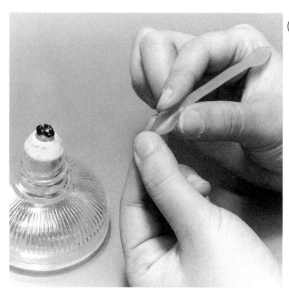

⑦ Gently curl the flower with fingers. Roll around the tapered portion of a pencil for a more pronounced curl at the base.

⑧ Use a pointed dowel, needle and spatula to create a variegated texture.

⑨ Melt small amounts of wax and deposit them along the edges to create additional texture. Be careful not to flow wax onto textured parts

Use a knife to cut serrated edges of the leaf. ⑩

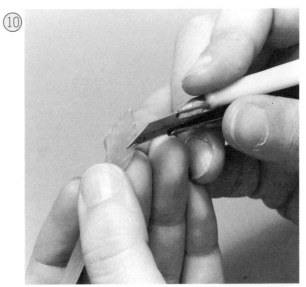

Heat a needle or knife to incise veins as on a natural leaf. ⑪

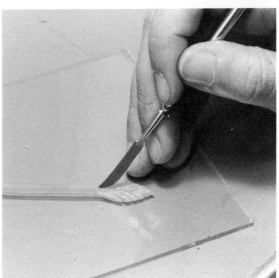

Coat ring mandrel with a film of light oil or talcum powder if a wood mandrel is used. ⑫

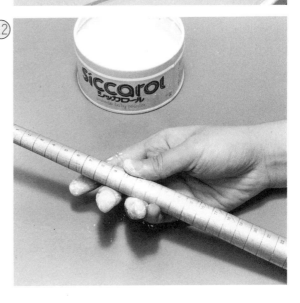

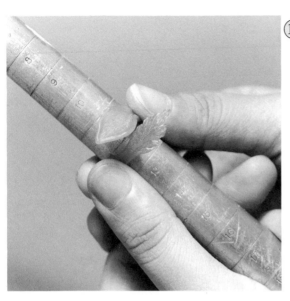

⑬ Bend the model around the mandrel at the proper ring size.

⑭ Remove the ring after sizing. Cross the leaf over the flower portion as shown.

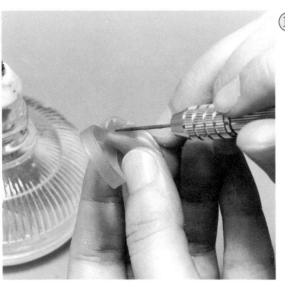

⑮ To stabilize the model, weld the cross over from the underside with additional wax. Clean up with cotton swab/wax solvent. Use sparingly.

COMMENTS :

Soft waxes may have a slight coating of talcum on the surface. A small amount of acetone or finger nail polish remover on a cotton swab will remove marking pen stains and powder. But precautions must be taken.

Although hard waxes are unaffected by acetone, soft waxes will melt slightly and textured surfaces will be affected by overuse. Use sparingly on such surfaces.

If the need arises, soft wax sheets may be reduced in thickness with a mandrel or rolling pin.

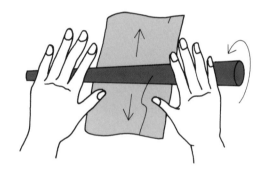

Thinly coat the sheet with talcum powder. Place it between sheets of paper.
Place the sandwich on a flat surface such as a 1/4" plate glass and roll lightly

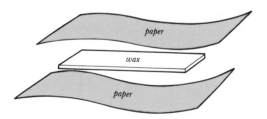

VARIATIONS OF THE FLOWER AND LEAF MOTIF

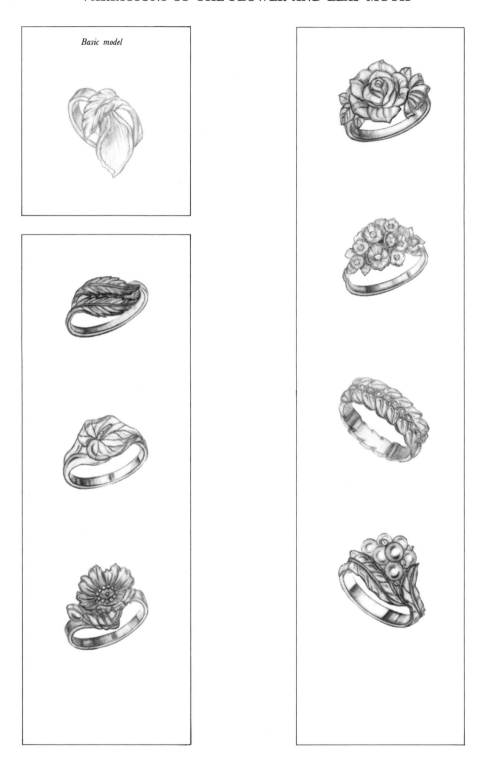

Basic model

POINT OF DESIGN Look for ideas in florae. Rings of this type can be constructed from one or more pieces with little effort due to the pliability of soft wax.

PROJECT NO. 10

A. LOZENGE PENDANT
WITH A CUT-OUT

Required: A sheet of soft wax 18 or 20 gauge.
Certain designs can be executed faster in the soft wax medium rather than using hard wax or metal. Hammered finish, bending, shaping and adding beads are readily accomplished.

2 views of the finished pendant

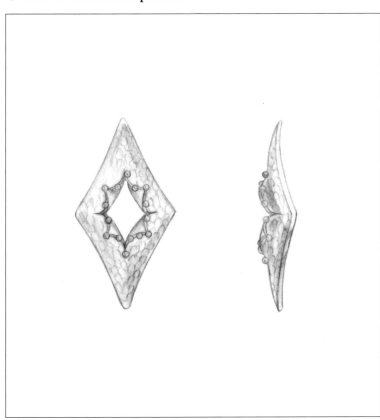

1. Draw the diamond outline centered about the perpendicular lines as shown. Place a sheet of glass over the drawing. Place an 18 or 20 gauge sheet of soft wax over the glass and cut out.

2. Cut cross slits at the perpendicular lines. Do not cut through completely. Finish cutting from the reverse side.

3. Push up and curl the slit portions as shown. Curl segments around a dowel for uniform curvature.

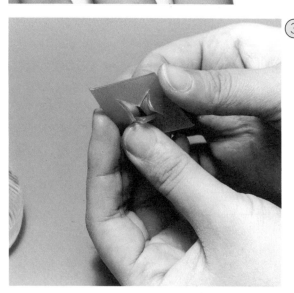

Warm a round blade carver or spatula and uniformly dent the surface with the underside of the tool to create a hammered texture. Try this on scrap material first. ④

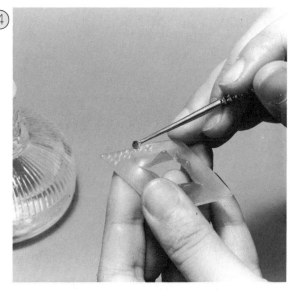

Trim the lozenge outline with a knife and finger burnish. ⑤

COMMENT:

Soft wax placed on a sheet of lightly crinkled aluminum foil and rolled with a mandrel offers an interesting texture.

Ring flanked by crinkled aluminum foil textured wax.

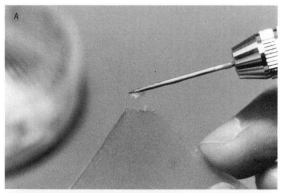

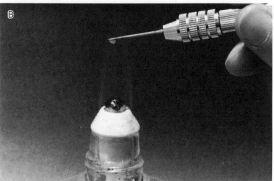

⑥ Small beads for attachment to the open frame of the lozenge may be made in the following manner. A small amount of wax is picked up on the tip of a needle. See "A". Heat the wax over the alcohol lamp. See "B".

Deposit the melted wax bead to the edge of the open frame. See "C".

If the wax is overheated, it will burn off. If the wax is not hot enough, it will not separate from the needle.

The bead may also flow onto the piece rather than beading up. Practice on a piece of scrap material.

Because of their light weight, wooden mandrels are handy for wax modeling. Mark ring sizes with a fine line pen.

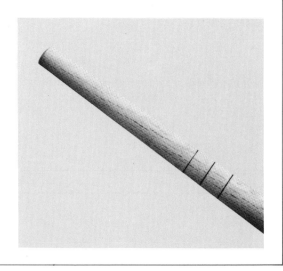

VARIATIONS OF THE CUT-OUT DESIGN

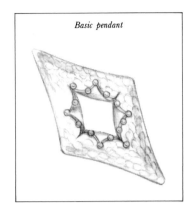

Basic pendant

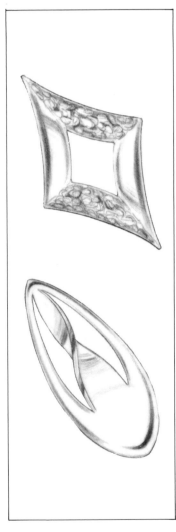

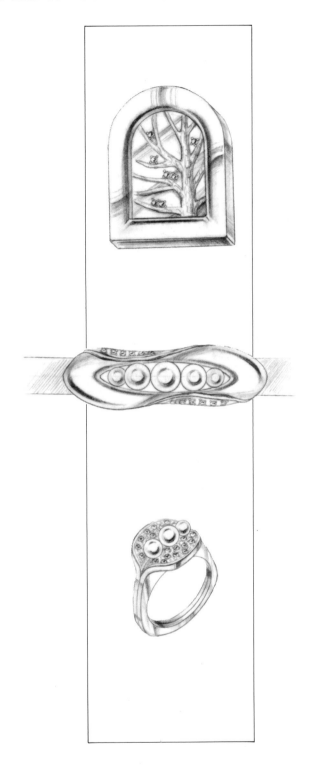

PROJECT NO 11

A BROOCH WITH A FLOWER
AND LEAVES

Required: A sheet of soft wax 22 or 24 gauge

Soft wax is an ideal medium for executing delicate designs, such as flowers and leaves.

The brooch consists of three entwined leaves and a flower. Since none of the pieces are shown in true size, paper cutouts may be necessary for length and width of the leaves. Trial fit the leaves and tack together with glue.

Examine the segments on the Step 6 photo for an idea of what they should like.

2 views of the finished pendant

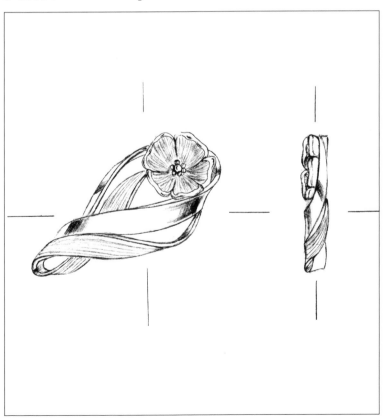

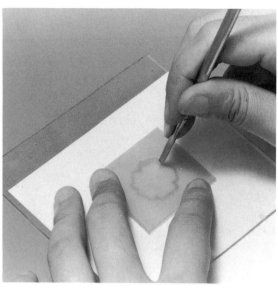

1 Sketch the flower larger than shown on the design. Place the sketch under a sheet of glass. Cut out the flower from a sheet of soft wax placed over the glass.

2 Curl the petals upward. Warm, if necessary. Use a suitable tool to aid in curling.

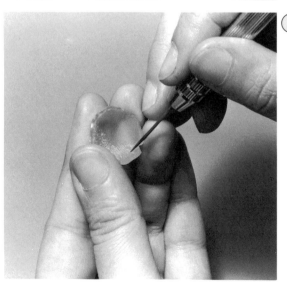

3 Add texture to the inside of the petals with a heated needle. Scribed lines should radiate from the center.

Use a needle or spatula and build up wax along the ④ edges of the petals to soften the appearance.

Place 6 or 7 beads of wax in the center of the ⑤ flower.

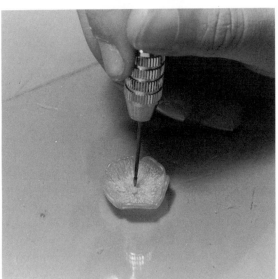

Draw the developed patterns for the three leaves. ⑥ Cover with a glass sheet. Place the wax sheet over the glass and cut to outline.

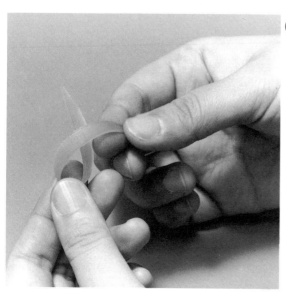

⑦ Warm the edges of the leaves over an alcohol lamp and finger burnish. Bend the leaves; shape as shown.

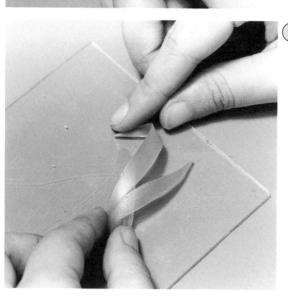

⑧ Add texture to the leaves; separate the cross-over to continue the texturing.

⑨ Arrange the leaves as shown on the design drawing; cutting and bending as required.

Check for over-all balance. Refer to the side view 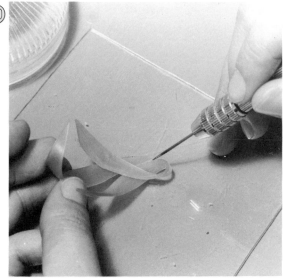 on the design drawing. Consider placement for the pin back. Weld, using sticky wax. Do not place any weld where it may be seen from the front.

Add the flower to the leaves. Weld from the reverse 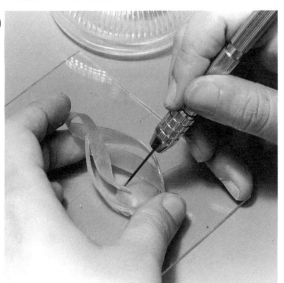 side.

COMMENTS:

Safe keeping and transporting delicate models.

Safe keeping

Place in a bowl of water.

Transporting

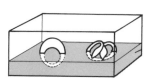

Place foam in a suitable container. Cut slits in foam.

Place model in a screw top jar filled with water.

VARIATIONS OF FLOWERS, FRONDS AND LEAVES

Basic model

POINT OF DESIGN Through imagination and experimentation, all types of jewelry can be created quickly once the technique of working with soft wax is mastered.

LOST WAX CASTING PROCESS

A BRIEF DESCRIPTION

While this book is devoted to creating wax models it is important for the modeler to know what takes place after the model is made.

There are many books written on casting and the wax modeler should familiarize himself with spruing techniques, investing and casting whether he does his own casting or not.

Models should be finished as smooth and faultless as possible since imperfections will be readily noticeable after the piece is cast, at which time repairs will be tedious to impossible.

A simple centrifugal machine is illustrated here, but other casting equipment -- vacuum and hand pressure units are used as well.

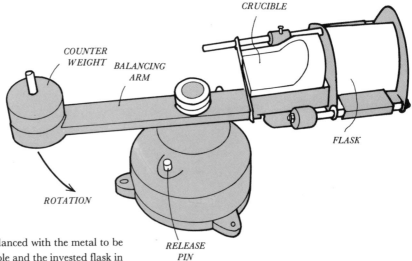

COUNTER WEIGHT

BALANCING ARM

CRUCIBLE

FLASK

ROTATION

RELEASE PIN

1. The casting machine is balanced with the metal to be melted placed in the crucible and the invested flask in the cradle.

2. The flask is placed in the burn-out furnace for the prescribed length of time. Shortly before removal time, the balance arm is rotated clockwise two or more times and held there by raising the release pin.

3. The metal is then melted with a torch. The flask is removed from the furnace and placed on the cradle. At the proper moment, the machine is allowed to spin causing the molten metal to enter the cavity left by the burned out wax.

FROM WAX MODEL TO METAL CASTING SIMPLIFIED

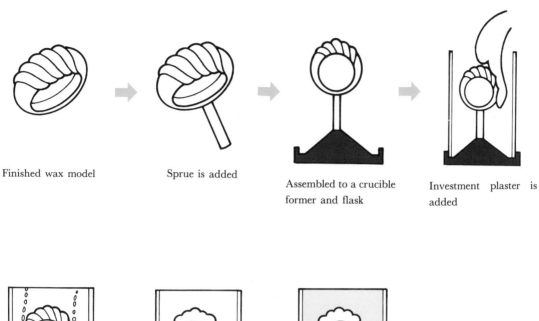

Finished wax model

Sprue is added

Assembled to a crucible former and flask

Investment plaster is added

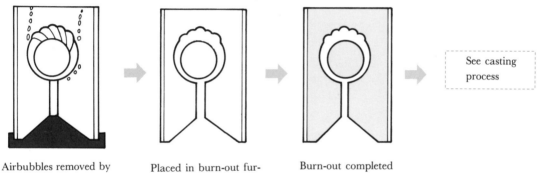

Airbubbles removed by vacuum or vibration

Placed in burn-out furnace

Burn-out completed

See casting process

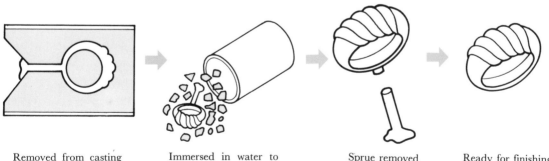

Removed from casting machine

Immersed in water to break up plaster

Sprue removed

Ready for finishing

APPENDIX

RING SIZE

Ring size	Diameter inches	Length inches	Ring size	Diameter inches	Length inches
0	0.458	1.4388	6 1/2	.666	2.0923
1/4	.466	1.4640	7	.682	2.1426
1/2	.474	1.4891	7 1/2	.698	2.1928
3/4	.482	1.5142	8	.714	2.2431
1	.490	1.5394	8 1/2	.730	2.2934
1 1/2	.506	1.5896	9	.746	2.3436
2	.522	1.6399	9 1/2	.762	2.3939
2 1/2	.538	1.6902	10	.778	2.4442
3	.554	1.7404	10 1/2	.794	2.4944
3 1/2	.570	1.7907	11	.810	2.5447
4	.586	1.8410	11 1/2	.826	2.5950
4 1/2	.602	1.8912	12	.842	2.6452
5	.618	1.9415	12 1/2	.858	2.6955
5 1/2	.634	1.9918	13	.874	2.7458
6	.650	2.0420	13 1/2	.890	2.7960

PLATE AND WIRE GAUGE COMPARISONS

B&S gauge	M/M	Inches	B&S gauge	M/M	Inches
4	5.189	.2043	16	1.290	.0508
6	4.111	.1620	18	1.024	.0403
8	3.264	.1285	20	0.813	.0320
10	2.588	.1019	22	0.643	.0253
12	2.052	.0808	24	0.511	.0201
14	1.629	.0641	26	0.404	.0159

WEIGHT CHART

Carat	Gram	Troy ounce	Troy pound	Avoird. ounce	Avoird. pound
1	0.2	0.00643	.000536	.007055	.000441
5	1	0.03215	.002679	.03527	.002205
155.517	31.1034	1	.083333	1.09714	.06857
1866.24	373.248	12	1	13.17	.8229
141.747	28.3495	0.9115	.07595	1	.0625
2267.95	453.59	14.583	1.215	16	1

MILLIMETER/INCH CONVERSION

M/M	decimal	INCH	fraction
1	.03937	.0625	1/16
2	.07874		
3	.11811	.125	1/8
4	.15748	.1875	3/16
5	.19685		
6	.23622	.250	1/4
7	.27559	.3125	5/16
8	.31496		
9	.35433	.375	3/8
10 (1cm)	.39370		
11	.43307	.4375	7/16
12	.47244	.500	1/2
13	.51181		
14	.55118	.5625	9/16
15	.59055	.625	5/8
16	.62992		
17	.66929	.6875	11/16
18	.70866		
19	.74803	.750	3/4
20 (2cm)	.78740	.8125	13/16
21	.82677		
22	.86614	.875	7/8
23	.90551	.9375	15/16
24	.94488		
*25	.98425	1.000	
26	1.02362		

*25.4mm=one inch

DIAMOND CARAT/DIAMETER TABLE

Carat wt.	Diameter millimeter	Carat wt.	Diameter millimeter
.01	1	.21	3 3/4
.02	1 1/4	.23	4
.03	1 1/2	.25	4 1/8
.04	1 3/4	.30	4 1/4
.05	2	.38	4 1/2
.06	2 1/4	.42	4 3/4
.08	2 1/2	.46	5
.09	2 3/4	.50	5 1/4
.11	3	.63	5 1/2
.13	3 1/8	.75	5 3/4
.15	3 1/4	.88	6
.19	3 1/2	1ct.	6 1/4

ABOUT THE AUTHOR

1970 Graduate of Rikkyo University
Director of Japan Jewelry Studies Institute
Member of The Japan Jewelry Designers Association

AUTHOR OF COMPANION BOOKS
"KAZARI Jewelry Technique",
"Practical Jewelry Design",
"Jewelry Engraving & Gem-setting",
"Practical Wax Modeling"

KASHIWA TECHNICAL BOOKS

PRACTICAL WAX MODELING -new revised ed.

Advanced Techniques for Wax Modelers

By Hiroshi Tsuyuki & Yoko Ohba

'99 Edition

Contents:
Model Making with Hard Wax
Model Making with Soft Wax and Beeswax
stone in wax technique
Applications of the Wax Technique
Casting Processes & Rubber-mold making 〈 new chapter 〉
Processing and Finishing after Casting

455 illustrations
Size 257mm × 182mm
Page 152
Available in English
Published by Matsubara-Kashiwa Books Inc.

JEWELRY BOOKS AVAILABLE FROM THE PUBLISHER

1. BASIC WAX MODELING by Hiroshi Tsuyuki $29.95
   120 pages *many photos* hardcover

2. PRACTICAL WAX MODELING by Hiroshi Tsuyuki   34.95
   152 pages *many photos* hardcover

3. AN ILLUSTRATED BOOK OF CAMEOS & GREEK MYTH by Mitsuhisa Maekawa   33.00
   176 pages *many photos in color* semi-hard

4. GEMSTONES—Quality & Value I by Yasukazu Suwa   92.00
   144 pages *full-color* hardcover

5. JEWELRY DESIGNS AT BELLE EPOQUE DE PARIS   20.00
   160 pages *fully illustrated* softcover

6. MODERN JAPANESE JEWELRY DESIGNS by Gyoshu Tashiro   25.00
   250 pages *fully illustrated* hardcover

7. QUALITY OF GEMSTONES BY Yasukazu Suwa   42.00
   56 pages *many photos in color* hardcover

8. CULTURED PEARLS by Andy Muller   60.00
   144 pages *full-color* hardcover

9. THE RING DESIGN 3900   85.00
   260pages *full-color* hardcover

10. JEWELRY SHOPS—Japan's best 200 shops selections   29.95
    254 pages *full-color* softcover

11. TOKYO JEWELERS magazine quarterly   single copy 16.00
    120 pages each issue *many photos in color*   subscription 100.00

ORDER ACCEPTED BY:

METALLIFEROUS INC., New York Tel(212)944-0909 Fax(212)944-0644

GIA BOOKSTORE, Carlsbad Tel(800)421-8161 Fax(760)603-4266

or MATSUBARA-KASHIWA BOOKS INC., Tokyo, Japan Fax +81-3353-4599